REDBACK publishing

AUSTRALIAN TRANSPORT

AIR TRANSPORT

ALISON HIDEKI

Redback Publishing
Suite 6, 13a Narabang Way,
Belrose NSW 2085
Australia

www.redbackpublishing.com
orders@redbackpublishing.com

ISBN 978-1-761401-57-2

Author: Alison Hideki
Editor: Marianne Lindsell
Designer: Redback Publishing

Original illustrations © Redback Publishing 2025
Originated by Redback Publishing

Acknowledgements
Abbreviations: l—left, r—right, b—bottom, t—top, c—centre, m—middle
We would like to thank the following for permission to reproduce photographs: (Images © shutterstock) p6m Box kite by Richtom80 via Wikimedia Commons, p7b Houdini airborne in his Voisin at Diggers Rest, March 1910, State Library NSW, p8b First England-Australia flight, Keith and Ross Smith, 1919 – Darwin, NT, State Library NSW, p8b Speeches of welcome from the assembled crowd. First England-Australia flight, Keith and Ross Smith, 1919 – Darwin, NT, State Library NSW, p24 Hawker-800XP2 by Eugene Butler via Wikimedia Commons.

A catalogue record for this book is available from the National Library of Australia

CONTENTS

AIR TRANSPORT TODAY

The distances between many towns and cities in Australia are great, so air transport is very important. It provides a fast and safe method of transporting people and goods long distances. Aeroplanes travel much faster than cars, buses, trucks, trains or ships, but they are more expensive to operate, so fares and rates are higher. Large quantities of goods are carried by other kinds of transport to keep costs low, and some things are too large to fit inside an aeroplane.

AIRLINE SERVICES

Major airlines such as Qantas, Jetstar, Virgin Australia and Tigerair Australia operate regular services between Australian towns and cities, and to overseas destinations. Australia also has numerous regional airlines such as FlyPelican and REX. Companies that specialise in airfreight, operate services between Australian towns and cities.

Aeroplanes and helicopters are also used for crop dusting, mustering livestock, search and rescue, police work, news gathering and for tourist joy flights.

Overseas airlines also operate services between Australia and other countries.

DOMESTIC AND INTERNATIONAL TRAVEL

There are two types of air transport: domestic and international. Domestic transport involves people or goods travelling within their own country. International transport involves people or goods travelling to or from another country.

LARGE AND SMALL

Aeroplanes range from small single engine aircraft that carry a pilot and several passengers to planes that can carry more than 500 passengers as well as the crew. Some aircraft are also set up to carry freight.

TRANSPORT

Transport is the movement of people or goods from one place to another. There are many kinds of transport, including airplanes, cars, trucks, ships, trains, pipelines and conveyor belts. Transport has always been very important for humans, as it makes it possible for people to communicate with one another, and to trade with one another.

FIRST FLIGHTS

Aviation in Australia began in 1858, when William Deane flew over Melbourne in a hot air balloon. In 1894 at Stanwell Park south of Sydney, inventor Lawrence Hargrave built a large box-kite. Hargrave flew in this to a height of five metres above the ground. This was the first recorded heavier-than-air flight in Australia.

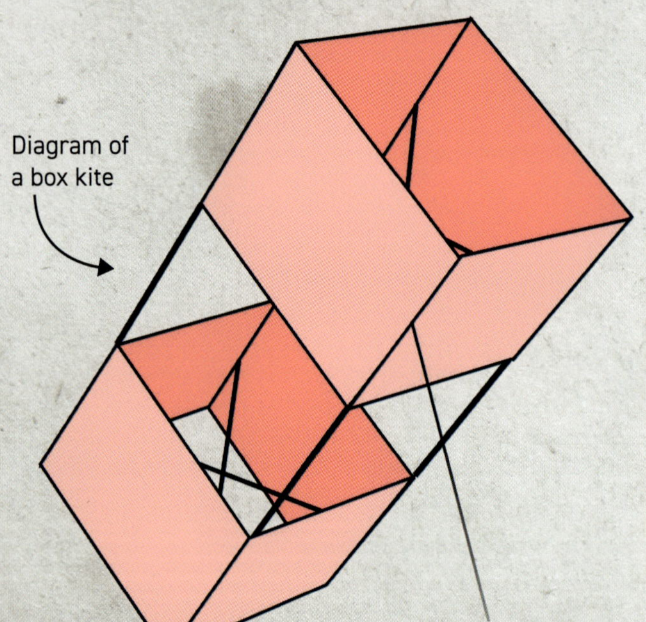

Diagram of a box kite

WORLD'S FIRST FLIGHTS

The first human flight was made in France more than 200 years ago. In 1783 in Paris, Jean Pilatre de Rozier and the Marquis d´Arlandes flew a hot air balloon made by Joseph and Etienne Montgolfier. They travelled nine kilometres. The first heavier-than-air powered flight was achieved by Orville and Wilbur Wright in the United States. Orville flew their plane a distance of nearly 40 metres, on December 17, 1903.

Wilbur just after landing the 1901 glider. Glider skid marks are visible behind it, and marks from a previous landing are seen in front

POWERED FLIGHTS

In 1909, Colin Defries flew a small aeroplane above Melbourne's Victoria Park raceway for five seconds, reaching a height of about five metres. He flew approximately 100 metres, but this was not far enough for the flight to be officially recognised as the first powered heavier-than-air flight in Australia. This honour was probably achieved in March 1910 by Frederick Custance of Adelaide, although some people doubted his claim. He flew for about 5 minutes and 30 seconds in a Bleriot monoplane (which had been shipped from France to Australia). He reached heights of five metres during his five kilometre flight.

Three days later, the world famous stuntman Harry Houdini (Erich Weiss) flew for 3 minutes and 30 seconds at Diggers Rest in Victoria and received great acclaim for the 'first' powered flight.

Four months later Victorian John Duigan flew the first Australian built powered aeroplane at Spring Plains, Victoria. He made the aeroplane using a petrol motor made in Melbourne, and followed the design of Hargrave's box-kite.

John Duigan at the Controls of his Biplane

Harry Houdini acheiving the 'first' powered flight, although he may not really have been the first.

FIRST PILOTS LICENCE

Australia's first licenced pilot was William Hart. He received his licence in 1911, and in 1912 he won an air race in Sydney against American 'Wizard' Stone. They took off from Botany, heading for Parramatta. Hart flew the 23 kilometres in just under 24 minutes to win the race. On the way he passed through two rain clouds. Stone became lost after flying out of a cloud, and flew in the wrong direction.

FAMOUS AVIATORS

At the beginning of the twentieth century Australians were keen to keep up good communication ties with Britain. There had been improvements in sea transport, and the link meant important messages could be sent between Australia and Europe. However air transport promised faster postal services and faster travel than travel by steamship.

Capt. Ross Smith (left) and observer with their Bristol F.2B Fighter

BRITAIN TO AUSTRALIA

Adelaide brothers Ross and Keith Smith joined Britain's Royal Air Force during World War I. When the war ended in 1918, they decided to fly back to Australia to try to win the £10,000 prize offered by the Australian Government for the first flight by an Australian crew from England to Australia. They set off from London in November 1919 in an old air force biplane. They took nearly 28 days to cover the distance with many stops along the way. They landed at Flemington Racecourse, Melbourne, in February 1920.

Ross and Keith Smith were welcomed at Darwin in December 1919 on their way to Melbourne, from London.

CHARLES KINGSFORD SMITH

Australia's most famous early aviator was Charles Kingsford Smith. With Charles Ulm, 'Smithy' broke many records and helped to set up Australia's airline industry. They made the first flight between the United States and Australia in 1928 in their famous three engine aeroplane, the Southern Cross. The journey took nine days. In 1934 Smith made the first flight from Australia to America in a single engine plane. Kingsford Smith disappeared near India on a flight from Britain to Australia in 1935.

BERT HINKLER

Australian aviator Bert Hinkler set out to break the Smith brothers' record for the fastest flight between England and Australia. In 1928 he covered the distance in 16 days, at the same time setting the record for the longest ever solo flight. Hinkler became a national hero. Sadly, he died in a plane crash in Italy in 1933.

WHAT'S THE DIFFERENCE?

Monoplanes have one wing on each side of the aeroplane's fuselage (body). Biplanes have two wings on each side, and triplanes have three. All modern planes are monoplanes.

THE FIRST AIRLINES

After the pioneering flights of early aviators such as the Smith brothers, people realised that air travel could be used for regular passenger and freight services.

QANTAS

In the Australian outback in the 1920s, roads were little more than rough tracks and railway lines only reached some places. Aeroplanes could easily cover the vast distances of the outback. In 1920, in the remote Queensland town of Winton, pilots Hudson Fysh and Paul McGinness formed the Queensland and Northern Territory Aerial Service (Qantas). They began flying between Charleville and Cloncurry, carrying mail, small parcels and passengers. They also took people on joy flights.

Arrival at Longreach of the Armstrong Whitworth FK8 with the first bag of air mail from Charleville to Cloncurry, 22 November 1922

Sydney airport today

FIRST AIRPORT

The first airfields were flat expanses of grass. Airports developed at airfields near towns and cities around Australia.

In 1919, one of the first airports used in Australia, was a cow paddock near the small town of Mascot, south of Sydney. It was officially declared an airport in 1921, the same year that Melbourne airport was established at Essendon. Today the Mascot airfield is the site of Kingsford Smith Airport, Sydney's international airport, and an airport still operates at Essendon. Brisbane airport was established at Eagle Farm in 1922.

AUSTRALIAN NATIONAL AIRLINES

During the 1920s other airlines were established. In 1930 Charles Kingsford Smith and Charles Ulm formed Australian National Airways (ANA), which operated the first regular air services between Brisbane, Sydney and Melbourne. It was now possible to travel between Brisbane and Melbourne in less than a day, a journey that would usually take more than a week by road or sea.

Australian National Airways aeroplane in flight 1950

INTERNATIONAL AIR SERVICES

After World War II, Qantas began overseas services to Fiji, Singapore and London. Qantas was bought by the Commonwealth Government in 1947, and for 46 years it was Australia's only international airline. New types of aeroplanes were larger and more reliable, and could travel longer between stops. This made air travel more attractive to people, although it was still very expensive when compared with sea transport.

PASSENGER SERVICE

Every year millions of people in Australia travel by air. Many of these are tourists and other visitors from overseas. In the 2016 to 2017 financial year, international passenger traffic reached over 38 million. Many more people travel domestically, within Australia, for business or holidays.

DOMESTIC ROUTES

Domestic routes link Australia's towns and cities, and tourist destinations. The busiest route is between Sydney and Melbourne. Major airlines also fly to Hobart, Canberra, Brisbane, Gold Coast, Adelaide, Perth, Cairns and Darwin. Less frequent services go to many smaller cities such as Kalgoorlie, Mackay, Wagga Wagga, Ballina/Byron and Mildura. Some of these routes are serviced by smaller airlines, operating smaller planes.

INTERNATIONAL ROUTES

Australia's international airlines are Qantas, Jetstar and Virgin Australia. Tiger Airlines also covers some destinations in Asia. They operate more than 550 international flights each week to places in Asia, Europe, North and South America, Africa and the Pacific.

About 60 international airlines operate scheduled services to and from Australia, including five freight airlines. There are also airlines that operate in Australia but only via code share arrangements with other airlines.

AIRLINES IN AUSTRALIA

For many years, the Commonwealth Government controlled the number of airlines that could operate on major routes such as Sydney to Melbourne, however that changed and other airlines began to compete with Qantas and (now defunct) Ansett on flights between the major cities.

A view inside the Boeing 787 Dreamliner

TYPES OF PLANES

The size and type of aircraft used on a route depends on the distance travelled and the number of people to be transported. For many years the Boeing 747 has been used for long international flights, but many airlines are now retiring this iconic plane. It is being replaced by more modern planes such as Boeing's 787 Dreamliner and Airbus models such as the enormous A380. Medium sized planes fly between Sydney and Melbourne. Smaller planes fly between capital cities and smaller regional cities and country towns.

WHO CONTROLS AIR TRANSPORT IN AUSTRALIA

Air travel within Australia and its surrounding area is controlled by Airservices Australia, which is operated by the Commonwealth Government. It is responsible for air traffic control (controlling the movements of aircraft), communication, search and rescue, and airport emergency services such as firefighting.

Airservices Australia employs more than 3,500 staff, including approximately 1,000 air traffic controllers. These air traffic controllers work from two air traffic services centres, two terminal control units and 29 towers at international and regional airports around Australia. Air traffic controllers manage the arrival and departure of more than 154 million airline passengers annually.

The Civil Aviation Safety Authority (CASA), also a Commonwealth Government organisation, is responsible for licensing pilots and airlines, making safety rules and inspecting aircraft and airports to make sure they are safe.

AIRMAIL AND AIRFREIGHT

Most freight is carried on ships, trains or semitrailers, but air transport is important when goods need to be transported quickly over long distances. However, air transport is much more expensive than other types of freight transport.

AIRMAIL

Airmail is one of the most important types of airfreight. Most mail between Australia and other countries is carried aboard aeroplanes, either in the cargo hold of passenger planes or aboard special freight planes. Airmail letters and parcels can be delivered to most places all over the world within a few days of being posted in Australia. Mail that travels aboard ships (called surface mail) can take weeks, or sometimes months, to arrive.

THE FIRST AIRMAIL

The first airmail was carried between Melbourne and Sydney in 1914 by Maurice Guillaux. He carried 1,785 letters. The trip took two and a half days, although the actual flying time was about eight hours. The same flight today takes about one hour. The first airmail service to England began in 1931.

A view inside a plane designed for carrying freight

SPECIAL FREIGHT

Other goods are carried by airfreight. Goods such as fresh flowers and seafood are sometimes exported by aeroplane. This is to make sure they arrive at their destination quickly, before they wilt or become stale. Gemstones such as opals and diamonds are also usually carried aboard aeroplanes, because they are very small and valuable.

FREIGHT PLANES

Usually, the same types of aeroplanes used to carry passengers are used to carry freight. But seats and other equipment are removed when carrying freight. Passenger planes can carry freight in the cargo hold. A medium sized aeroplane may carry as much as 10 tonnes of freight in the cargo hold, under the floor of the passenger compartment. This part of the plane also holds all the passengers' baggage.

AUSTRALIAN AIRPORT

There are about 615 airports in Australia. They range from large international airports that handle thousands of passengers every day to tiny airfields in small country towns. Most airports are owned by local councils, State Governments, the Department of Defence (air force bases) or private companies.

INTERNATIONAL AIRPORTS

Flights from overseas must land at one of Australia's international airports. Australia's main international airports are:

- Sydney
- Brisbane
- Cairns
- Darwin
- Melbourne
- Perth
- Adelaide
- Gold Coast

There are also a number of other airports with restricted international use. All these airports have to check that no illegal goods are brought into the country, and that customs duties (taxes) are paid. Immigration officials also check passengers' passports.
Some of the many airlines that fly into Australia are:

- Singapore Airlines
- Air China
- China Eastern
- Air New Zealand
- Qatar Airways
- Etihad Airways
- Cathay Pacific
- Thai Airways
- Malaysia Airways
- Eva Air
- Garuda Indonesia
- ANA (All Nippon Airways)
- Vietnam Airlines
- Asiana Airlines
- Philippine Airlines
- Japan Airlines
- Korean Air
- Emirates

OTHER AIRPORTS

Most large country towns and regional cities have an airport with air services to the nearest state capital city and to other regional cities. Large cities such as Sydney and Melbourne have a number of airports. The busiest airport in Australia, in terms of the number of take offs and landings each day, is Bankstown Airport in Sydney. Flights to and from Bankstown are mainly in privately owned light aircraft and commercial flights from very small towns.

In July 2017, there were 5.49 million passengers carried on Australian domestic commercial aviation (including charter operations). The top three airports for passenger movements were:

Sydney - 2.37 million
Melbourne - 2.22 million
Brisbane - 1.56 million

A further 2.21 million domestic passengers moved through regional airports.

AT THE AIRPORT

Large airports have at least one runway, taxiways, a control tower, a terminal building for arriving and departing passengers, and hangars. There are also buildings where inflight meals are prepared, as well as administration offices.

AIR TRAFFIC CONTROL

All aeroplane pilots have to obey radio instructions from air traffic controllers, who watch aeroplane movements on screens. Air traffic controllers work in control towers where they can keep track of the movements of aeroplanes on the taxiways and runways, as well as aeroplanes approaching the airport.

TERMINAL OPERATIONS

Once an aeroplane has landed and has taxied close to the terminal building, a small powerful vehicle called a tug pulls it to the correct gate. The tug pulls the plane using a metal rod attached to the aeroplane's front landing gear. Tugs also push aeroplanes away from the terminal before the aircraft move along taxiways to take off. Aircraft are refuelled by tanker trucks that pump fuel into the aeroplanes' fuel tanks. At some large airports, mobile pumps transfer fuel to the planes from underground pipes.

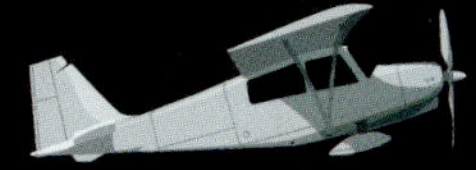

BAGGAGE HANDLING

Millions of bags and parcels pass through major airports every week. Each item of luggage is marked with the flight number and its destination, to make sure that baggage handlers put it on the correct aeroplane. Baggage handlers also unload each aeroplane. They put the bags on large conveyer belts called carousels, from where passengers collect them.

AIRCRAFT SERVICES AND MAINTENANCE

Huge buildings called hangars house aircraft for cleaning, repair and maintenance. All aircraft are checked regularly for faults to avoid accidents.

IMMIGRATION AND CUSTOMS

Passengers and baggage pass through X-ray machines and metal detectors that scan for firearms and other dangerous goods. Customs officers and immigration officials at international airports check passengers' identities, as well as checking their luggage for illegal goods.

HOW AN AEROPLANE WORKS

PARTS OF AN AEROPLANE

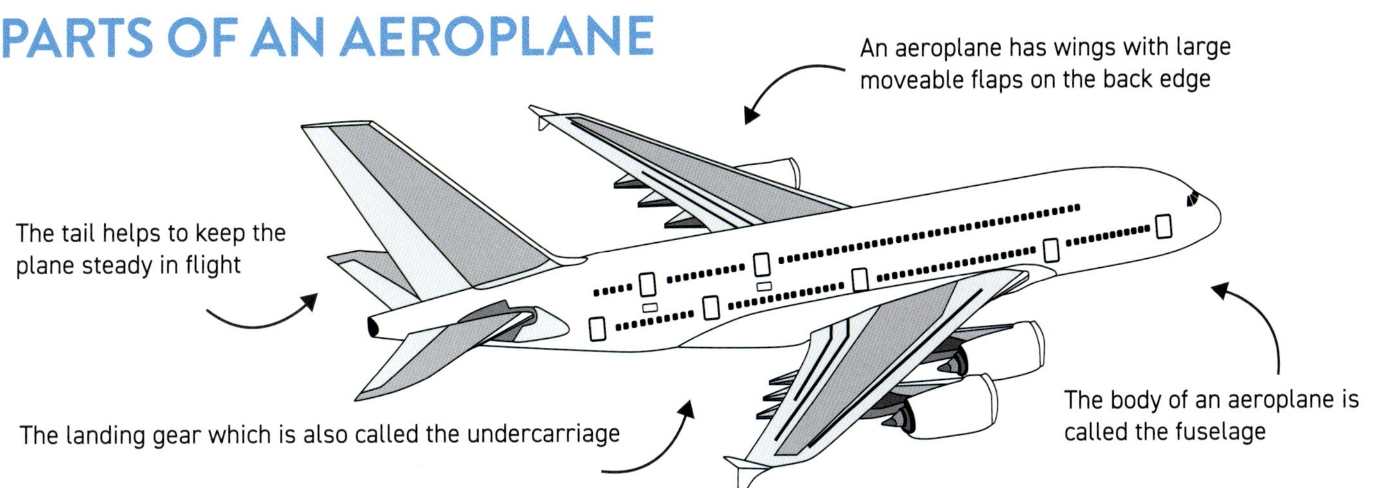

HOW A PLANE FLIES

An aeroplane rises into the air due to the flow of air over and under its wings. The wings are lower at the rear (trailing) edge than the front (leading) edge. As the plane is pushed forwards by the engine, air passing under the wing is pushed downwards, which forces the wing upwards. This is known as lift. The amount of lift depends on the shape, area and angle of the wing, and how fast the air is flowing across the wings.

TAKING OFF AND LANDING

Aeroplanes usually take off into the wind. This increases the flow of air across the wing, helping the pilot control the plane. As an aeroplane approaches the airport, the plane slows and the landing gear is lowered. As soon as the plane touches down, the engines are reversed. This brings the plane to a halt.

On take off, the aeroplane accelerates along the runway until it is travelling fast enough for the flow of air over and under the wings to cause it to rise into the air. Flaps on the wings are lowered, to give the plane extra lift.

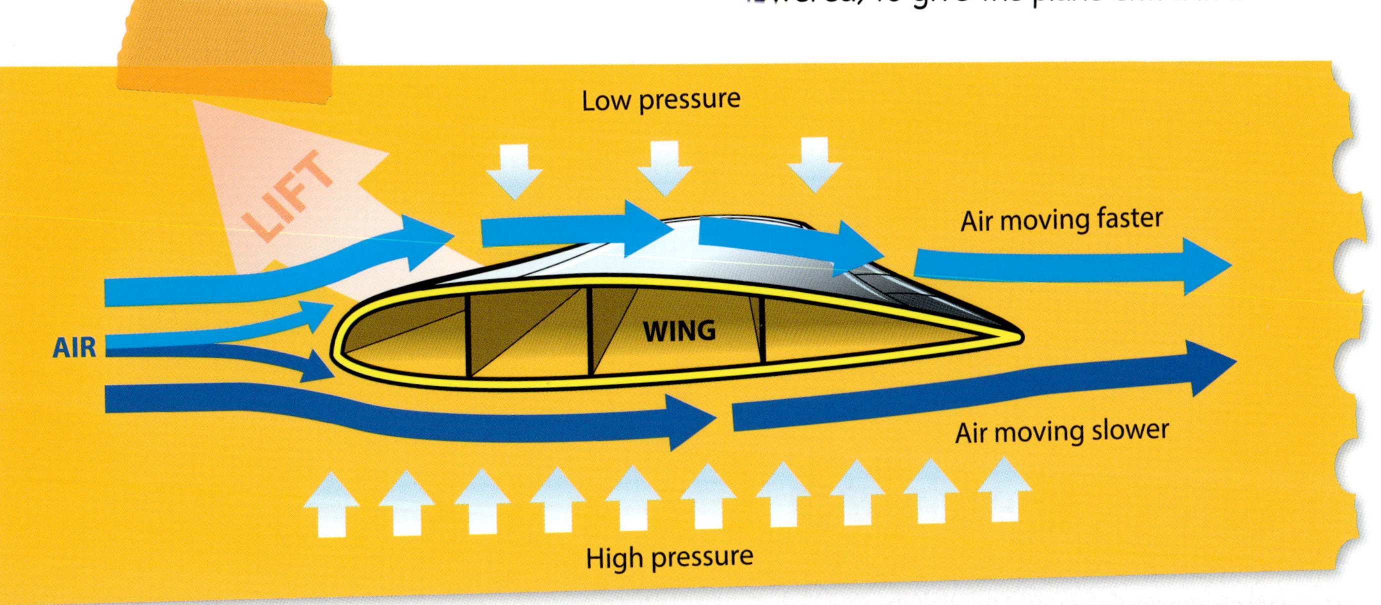

A jet engine from an aeroplane

TYPES OF ENGINES

Aeroplanes are powered either by propellers or by jet propulsion. In a propeller-driven aeroplane, an internal combustion engine (similar to a car engine) turns a propeller, which forces air backwards, making the plane move forwards.

Jet engines rely on burning fuel. In a turbojet, hot gases from burning fuel are forced from the rear of the engine, making the plane move forwards. Turbofan engines combine the force of the moving gases with a large fan, which works in a similar way to a propeller. Turbofan engines are quieter than other types of jet engines.

IN THE COCKPIT

In the cockpit, the pilot and the copilot use a control stick, levers and foot pedals to control the movements of the wing flaps and other parts of the plane. They can make it change direction or gain or lose height, and control the amount of power produced by the engines.

SAFETY IN THE AIR

Australia has an excellent international air safety record. Domestic flights are also very safe. Air crashes in Australia claim about 50 lives a year. Most of these crashes involve light (small) planes.

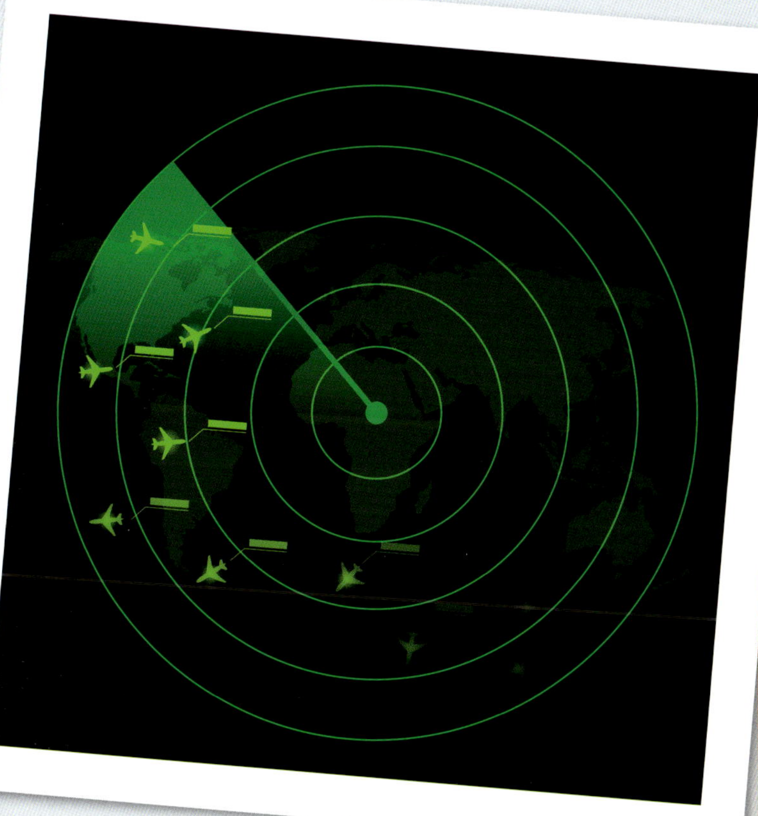

AIR TRAFFIC CONTROL

Air traffic controllers make sure aeroplanes stay well clear of each other, and that they are flying by the safest and most direct route. They use radio and radar to keep track of the thousands of aircraft flying in Australian skies.

THE BLACK BOX

The black box helps investigators work out why air crashes happen. It contains electronic equipment that records conversations between the pilot and copilot, and other information about the flight. The box is bright orange, and made from very strong, fireproof material so that it has a good chance of remaining intact in the event of a crash. The black box on a Jumbo Jet is positioned near the tail, which is often the part of the plane least damaged in a crash.

IN-FLIGHT SAFETY

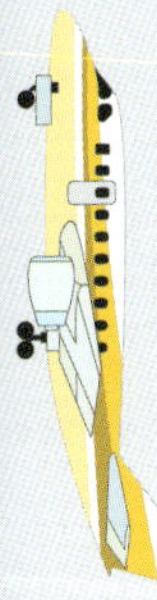

As an aeroplane taxis to the runway, flight attendants instruct passengers on what to do in an emergency, and how to use safety equipment such as oxygen masks and lifejackets. They also show the location of emergency exits. Passengers are not allowed to smoke aboard aeroplanes.

AIRCRAFT MAINTENANCE

All aircraft are checked regularly, and aeroplanes are completely overhauled every five years. Before every take off, the pilot and copilot do a final check of the instruments and the exterior of the plane.

SEARCH AND RESCUE

If a plane crashes, it must be located quickly. Air traffic controllers keep track of aircraft positions, and can direct rescue teams in road vehicles, helicopters or aeroplanes to the area of the crash. Most aircraft are fitted with ELT (emergency locater transmitters), which lead searchers to the crash site.

Australia's busiest airports have fulltime firefighters who are trained to fight fires in crashed aircraft. They also train local fire brigades, who are responsible for safety at smaller airports.

Satellite tracking allows air traffic controllers to keep track of aircraft movements.

Satellite tracking allows air traffic controllers to keep track of aircraft movements.

THE ROYAL FLYING DOCTOR SERVICE

The vast distances between small outback towns and properties means that many people living there don't have easy access to services such as hospitals and schools.

Until 1920, camels, horses and cars and trucks that rattled over rough dirt tracks were the only forms of transport in the outback. There were no radios, so messages could not be sent quickly. If there was a medical emergency, help could take some time to arrive.

TYPES OF AIRCRAFT

The first aeroplane used by the Royal Flying Doctor Service was a De Havilland 50A provided by Qantas. It had space for two stretchers.

Today the 66 plane fleet consists of several different types of aircraft, including the:

- Hawker 800XP
  (used in WA and NT)
- Pilatus PC-12
  (used in SA/NT and WA)
- King Air B350 C and B200 C
  (used in Qld, NSW, Victoria and Tasmania)
- Cessna C208
  (used in Qld)
- Pilatus PC-24 jets will be used in WA, SA and NT by 2018

One of the original De Havilland DH.50 machines used by the RFDS

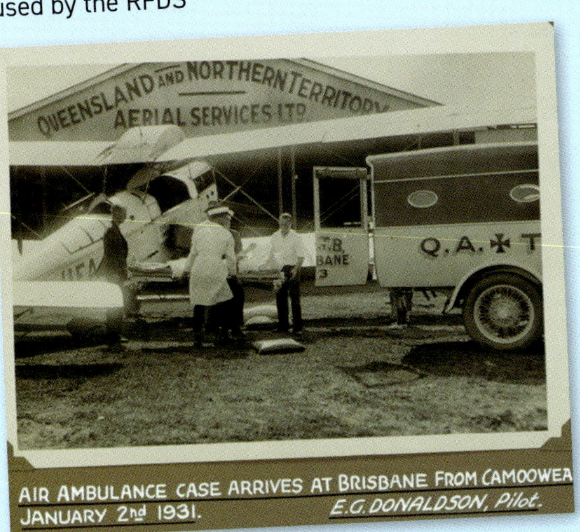

Reverend John Flynn appears on Australia's twenty dollar note

REVEREND JOHN FLYNN

During the 1920s, radios and aeroplanes became more dependable and widely used. In 1925 Reverend John Flynn, who worked for the Australian Inland Mission, began installing wirelesses (radios) in remote areas. He opened a wireless station in the Northern Territory. People could now radio for help in an emergency, and could keep in contact with their neighbours. There was no electricity supply in outback areas, so the first radios were powered by pedal generators.

THE FLYING DOCTOR

The Royal Flying Doctor Service provides health care and 24-hour emergency service to people over an area of 7.69 million square kilometres.

The first Royal Flying Doctor Service base (then known as the Aerial Medical Service) was opened at Cloncurry in central Queensland in 1928. Pedal wirelesses were given to stations and missions up to 550 kilometres away. In 1934, the service was extended to Western Australia with a base at Port Hedland. It continued to expand until it covered most of inland Australia.

Today the Royal Flying Doctor Service has 1,200 staff operating from 23 bases. The service provides regular clinics in remote areas not served by a resident doctor, and first aid kits to remote homesteads and Aboriginal communities, as well as emergency medical help, and transport to hospital.

A Hawker 800XP2 Royal Flying Doctor Service at Broome Airport

WORKING IN THE AIR INDUSTRY

Air traffic controllers control the movements of aeroplanes to make sure they do not collide or crash. They work at Australia's major airports. There are three types of air traffic controllers. En route controllers control planes flying over the Australian mainland and the oceans around Australia. They use radar and radio to keep track of their positions and altitudes, and to give pilots instructions and weather information.

En route controllers are employed at main centres in Brisbane and Melbourne.

Terminal area controllers control planes arriving and departing from large city airports at Cairns, Brisbane, Coolangatta, Sydney, Melbourne, Adelaide and Perth. They also manage light aircraft and helicopter movements in the same areas.

Tower controllers control planes on taxiways and runways from airport control towers around Australia. They clear planes to take off and land.

PILOTS

Pilots are trained at flying schools. After gaining a licence to fly light aircraft, pilots can undergo further training to fly larger planes. A commercial licence allows pilots to be employed flying joy flights, crop dusting, flying charter flights and flying for small airlines.

To fly large aircraft, a pilot usually has university qualifications in science and mathematics, and many hours flying experience. Some airline pilots begin flying in the air force. The captain is the main pilot of an aeroplane.

Flight attendants are trained in safety procedures and passenger service.

FLIGHT ATTENDANTS

Flight attendants (or cabin crew) are important for passenger comfort and safety. They serve meals, look after special passengers such as children travelling by themselves, elderly people and disabled people, and make passengers aware of safety routines. Many flight attendants speak more than one language.

EMERGENCY SERVICES

Firefighters and rescue workers at major airports are ready if there is an accident. They also provide first aid services and fire protection of airport buildings. Workers are trained in firefighting techniques and the operation of equipment such as fire extinguishers and fire engines. Firefighters also have to exercise regularly to keep fit, and have to pass a fitness test to be employed.

FLIGHT IN THE FUTURE

It wasn't long ago that the aeroplane was a cloth and timber kite with a tiny motor that struggled to rise five metres above the ground. Today's modern jet airliners can carry hundreds of passengers, and sleek military planes can travel at more than twice the speed of sound. Aeroplane manufacturers such as Boeing and Airbus are continually looking for ways to make aeroplanes more efficient and able to carry more passengers over greater distances.

QUIETER TAKE OFFS AND LANDINGS

With many airports in cities, noise pollution is a major concern. People who live near airports are concerned about noise levels in their environment. Newer engine designs have reduced the amount of noise produced by aeroplanes as they take off and land. In the future, quieter engines will be developed so people living near airports are not bombarded by noise.

In the future, quieter engines may lessen the problem of noise pollution from aircraft.

FAST FACT

Boeing predicts demand for 41,000 new commercial aircraft and 617,000 pilots over the next 20 years.

GET READY FOR

Air transport will evolve over the coming years. Some of the advances might include:

Flat Pack planes: fold these planes away after your flight.

Benches and standing room: these flights take budget travel to a new altitude.

Electric planes with fuel-cells as the main or auxiliary power system.

Companies that use planes in a similar way to today's cruise ships, taking passengers from one destination to another.

NASA is working on designs for planes that fly up to 85% of the speed of sound; cover a range of approximately 11,000 kilometers; and carry between 22 and 45 tonnes of payload, either passengers or cargo.

FIND OUT MORE

PRIMARY AND SECONDARY SOURCES

A primary source is information created by someone who was a part of or witnessed the historical event first hand. Primary sources are very important to historians researching events and time periods. Examples of primary sources are letters, emails, filmed interviews and clips, journals and diaries, census statistics, government documents, art and maps (from the time period), the news (both print and film), photographs and maps.

A secondary source is when someone who did not actually witness the event retells the facts that someone else told them. Examples of secondary sources include news (both print and film), interviews, letters, journals and diaries, biographies, textbooks and paraphrased quotations.

SEARCH KEY WORDS

Airlines
Boeing
Flight Tracker
Airbus
Sydney Airport
Royal Flying Doctor Service

PRIMARY AND SECONDARY SOURCES SEARCH

In 2008, Qantas was the third airline to put the A380 into commercial service.

Can you find some primary and secondary sources for this event?

FIND OUT MORE

To find out more about air transport in Australia visit the websites below, and to learn more about other types of transport take a look at more books in this series:

WEBSITES

AIRSERVICES AUSTRALIA

www.airservices.gov.au

BOEING COMPANY

www.boeing.com

CASA

www.casa.gov.au

VIRGIN AUSTRALIA

www.virginaustralia.com

QANTAS AIRLINES

www.qantas.com

JETSTAR AIRWAYS

www.jetstar.com

ROYAL FLYING DOCTOR SERVICE:

https://www.flyingdoctor.org.au

GLOSSARY

Accelerate go faster

Altitude height above sea level

Aviator a person who flies aeroplanes

Biplane an aeroplane with two wings on each side

Cargo hold the space under the floor of the passenger compartment, used to store freight and passenger baggage

Carousel a belt that moves continuously in a loop

Control Tower tall building where air traffic controllers watch aircraft movements

Customs officers people who inspect goods coming in to the country to ensure all tariffs and customs duties have been paid

Domestic domestic within Australia

Flight attendant a person who looks after passengers on airline flights

Freight goods sent by rail, road, sea or air

Fuselage the body of an aeroplane

Gate a part of an airport terminal where aircraft 'park' so passengers can embark and disembark

Hangar a large building for storing and repairing aircraft

Landing gear the wheels and supports used when a plane takes off or lands

Licence an official certificate that gives permission to do something

Maintenance keeping in good working order

Monoplane an aeroplane with one wing on each side of the fuselage

Navigation directing the course of an aircraft

Radar a device that shows the position and speed of an object by measuring the time the echoes of radio waves take to come back (formed from the words Radio Detection and Ranging)

Runway a level strip of land for aircraft to take off and land

Satellite an object that moves around a larger object in space. Satellites receive signals from one part of the Earth's surface and send them to another part of the Earth's surface.

Taxi the movement of an aeroplane along a runway before taking off and after landing

Telegraph a system that sends messages by sending electric signals along wires

Undercarriage landing gear

INDEX